WHITEFIELD

——— J.C. RYLE ———

WHITEFIELD

FOREWORD BY TOM J. NETTLES

H&E
Publishing

CONTENTS

Publisher's Note

In this edition, the punctuation and capitalization have been modernized, some archaic words have been updated, and a few other slight editorial changes made. Any significant changes note the original in the footnotes.

Acknowledgments

Thank you, Bennett Rogers and Tom Nettles for your contribution to this work. Also many thanks Benjamin Inglis and Ronald Heyboer for proofreading, and Chidera Orji for your help in transcription.

WHO IS J.C. RYLE

(1816–1900)?

By Bennett W. Rogers

J.C. Ryle was born and raised in a wealthy but unspiritual home.[1] He distinguished himself academically and athletically at Eton and Oxford. He experienced an evangelical conversion in his final year at university, the account of which has achieved a semi-legendary status among evangelicals—a testimony to the power of the public reading of Scripture.[2] Shortly thereafter, his

---

[1] For a life of Ryle, see Eric Russell, *J.C. Ryle: That Man of Granite with the Heart of a Child* (Fearn, Scotland: Christian Focus Publications, 2008); John Murray, Iain H. Murray, *J.C. Ryle: Prepared to Stand Alone* (Edinburgh, UK: Banner of Truth Trust, 2016); or my new intellectual biography of Ryle entitled *John Charles Ryle: The Man, His Ministry, and His Message* (Grand Rapids: Reformation Heritage Books, 2018).

[2] Around the time of his examinations, John Charles attended Carfax Church, formally known as St. Martin's, feeling somewhat depressed and discouraged. The reader of the lesson made some lengthy pauses when he came to verse 8: "By grace—are ye saved—

father's bankruptcy ruined the family, ended his political career before it started, and forced him into the ministry of the Church of England. Although he initially became a clergyman because he felt "shut up to it," Ryle quickly gained a reputation for being a powerful preacher, diligent pastor, popular author, and effective controversialist. He rose through the evangelical ranks to become the undisputed leader and party spokesman—the first to hold that distinction since Charles Simeon (1759-1836). He became the first Bishop of Liverpool in 1880 at an age (64) when many clergymen contemplate retirement, and served as the chief pastor of the second city of the British Empire until his death in 1900.

Ryle is probably best remembered as a writer of tracts, commentaries, and devotional works, and deservedly so. His tracts continue to be distributed. His commentaries on the gospels—Expository Thoughts on the Gospels—are still read by pastors and laymen alike. His practical writings, such as Old Paths, Practical Religion, and the Upper Room have remained popular with evangelical readers for well over a century. And Holiness: Its Nature, Hindrances, Difficulties, and Roots has become a modern spiritual classic. J. C. Ryle was also keenly interested in church history. In fact, he wrote twenty-five short biographies of important figures in

---

through faith—and that, not of yourselves—it is the gift of God." This unusual and emphatic reading of Ephesians 2:8 made a tremendous impact on him and led to his own evangelical conversion.

English church history and published a number of popular historical works about the English Reformation.[3] Ryle believed that church history is not merely interesting—it is instructive. It is nothing less than "philosophy teaching by examples." And no period of church history was more instructive than the 16th, 17th, and 18th centuries.

At the beginning of the sixteenth century, Roman Catholicism reigned supreme, and as a result, the land was engulfed in darkness. The vast majority of the English people lived in a miserable state of spiritual ignorance, monstrous superstition, degrading priestcraft, and gross immorality. The Bible was outlawed. Divine worship was unintelligible. Essential Christian doctrine was lost. Biblical holiness was unknown. In short, "there was an utter famine of vital Christianity in the land."[4] The Protestant Reformation delivered England from all these evils. It gave Englishmen the Bible in their own language and permission to read it. It made religious

---

[3] Ryle wrote biographical sketches of the following persons: George Whitefield, John Wesley, William Grimshaw, William Romaine, Daniel Rowlands, John Berridge, Henry Venn, Samuel Walker, James Hervey, Augustus Toplady, Fletcher of Madeley, John Wycliffe, John Rogers, John Hooper, Rowland Taylor, Hugh Latimer, John Bradford, Nicholas Ridley, Samuel Ward, Archbishop Laud, Richard Baxter, William Gurnall, James II and the Seven Bishops, Thomas Manton, and Colonel Robert Holden. For Ryle's works on the English Reformation see: *Lessons from English Church History*, *What Do We Owe the Reformation*, and *Why Were Our Reformers Burned*.

[4] J. C. Ryle, *Lessons from English Church History* (London: William Hunt and Company, 1871), 11.

worship simple, beautiful, and above all, intelligible. It revived the true teaching and preaching of the gospel, as well as the true standard of practical holiness. Ryle considered the Protestant Reformation of the sixteenth century to be the greatest blessing God ever bestowed on his country. And he regarded the martyred English Reformers, like Bishop Hugh Latimer, to be the best churchmen who ever lived.

In the seventeenth century, a party led by Archbishop Laud, began to reverse the work of the reformation and un-protestantize the Church of England. These Laudian divines began to exalt the Supper, ceremonies, and the episcopacy, and disparage the Reformers, the Puritans, and Calvinism. The consequences of this departure from the principles of the Reformation was, in a word, disastrous. It alienated many Englishmen from the Church of England and essentially created English Dissent. It led to a bloody civil war and the temporary destruction of the Church of England. And after the Restoration and the passage of the Act of Uniformity, it forced out two thousand of England's most able and holy ministers in the Great Ejection, including the famous pastor of Kidderminster, Richard Baxter.

In the years that followed, English Christianity began to die a slow death. Natural theology, cold morality, and barren orthodoxy took root in Church and chapel. Infidelity and skepticism became popular, even fashionable. The bishops and clergy of the Church of

England were worldly and ineffective. The Nonconformists won their religious liberty but lost their religious zeal. Immorality – dueling, drunkenness, and adultery – abounded. And the evangelical activism that would characterize that closing decades of the eighteenth century were nonexistent. But in the midcentury English Christianity was rescued and revived by the evangelical revival. The leaders of this Great Awakening, like George Whitefield, turned the nation upside down through their preaching and evangelism. They proclaimed the doctrine of the Puritans and the Reformers simply, fervently, and ubiquitously, and as a result, English Christianity was saved from the brink.

Hugh Latimer, Richard Baxter, and George Whitefield represent the best men and ministers of their respective ages. They show us what great influence one man can have on his generation when he has the truth on his side. J. C. Ryle was convinced that the Church of his day needed more bishops like Latimer, more pastors like Baxter, and more preachers like Whitefield. Though more than 160 years have passed since Ryle first published these biographical sketches, the need for such men remains unchanged. May these biographies inspire a new generations of Latimers, Baxters, and Whitefields.

FOREWORD

Tom J. Nettles

The Bishop of Liverpool demonstrated himself to be a steady devotee of the established church of England and, at the same time, an uncompromising evangelical. These lectures on George Whitefield demonstrate both of these life commitments for Ryle and contain an urgent defense of the one as well as the other.

He had no delusions about the condition of the Anglican church during the Georgian period. His summaries of that condition in these lectures are ruthlessly honest, clearly stated, and illustrated by pithy notations of the famous and influential during this period. Ryle accepted the idea that the Evangelical Awakening of the eighteenth century saved England from a social and political upheaval on the lines of the French Revolution. In his estimation, George Whitefield was the most effective preacher and had the most salubrious influence on the church and society of any of the evangelicals of the century. "I have come to the conclusion," Ryle wrote after extensive thought and consideration of Whitefield's life, energetic activity, and constant preaching, "that Whitefield was one of the most powerful and extraordinary preachers the world has ever seen." Whitefield has never been "too highly estimated," he argued and was willing to state categorically, "No living preacher ever possessed such a combination of excellences as Whitefield." Whitefield's detractors were little more than "shams and imposters" in their profession of Christianity and were therefore, unworthy "to be called church men at all."

What were Whitefield's excellencies? Those factors that gave him contact with the thousands upon thousands started with his unrelenting devotion to reach people. He would preach in church, cathedral, chapel, open field, in the street, or in a market place. He would go to Scotland, Wales, America, and everywhere in England to give his message. When he found them, they stayed to hear, for his voice was eminently attractive and people could listen with ease and never tire of his perfection of inflection and tone whether soft or strong. His impeccable linguistic skill and natural gift at rhetoric kept up the attention of the most critical from an oratorical standpoint and the least disposed to listen from a theological standpoint.

Given these gifts, the most critical aspect of his influence was his message. He himself had experienced a profound conversion and he desired the same—an intense desire salted with tears—for those who heard him. He preached a message that was uncompromising in its presentation of human sin and corruption, the necessity of redemption by Christ and justification by faith, the necessity of utter renovation of heart and affections by the Holy Spirit, the sovereign prerogative of God in bestowing these on his elect, and the inevitable consequence of a holy life for the truly converted.

Ryle's estimation of the importance of Whitefield had other anchors also. Whitefield preached evangelical truth purposefully affirming such content as consistent with the Thirty-nine Articles, the Book of Common Prayer, and the consent of history of the Church of England. Only two years prior to Ryles's delivery of this address, a widely contested and contentious case had appeared in both the ecclesiastical courts and the courts of state. These hearings culminated with an affirmation of the legitimacy of G. C. Gorham's appointment to the vicarage of Brampford Speke. Gorham's Calvinistic views were challenged as heterodoxy, but his high church challengers lost in their attempts to have him excluded. This case combined with the great change in the church as a result of Whitefield and other awakening preachers made the condition of the state church in Ryle's day far more acceptable and true to the biblical principle of Protestantism than it had been in the one hundred years before. None of the men to whom Ryle was speaking, therefore, should be tempted to become a

Dissenter, he urged, but must remain loyal to the established church.

It was this conviction of Ryle that made Charles Spurgeon say that, when faced with the reality of dissent, even an evangelical Anglican like Ryle can "put on priestly airs." Spurgeon called Ryle himself, "good, very good," but also said that his "churchianity is bad, very bad." It is understandable that as the leading voice among evangelical, Calvinistic Dissenters contemporary with Ryle, he would find him both lovely in ministry and enigmatic in his devotion to an established Christianity. Spurgeon had studied the history of the persecution of Baptists in England by the state church and found an evangelical defense of this mongrelized attempt at Christianity impossible. Ryle believed, however, that disestablishment would throw England into chaos.

Ryle's love for edifying historical figures should be an encouragement and a model for every minister of the gospel. He held before himself the most faithful and evangelical of the ministers of the past. He loved them and, thus, he became like them. His practice of learning the strengths of effective men, in examination of both the cost and the joy of uncompromising fidelity to Christ and his gospel should be a consistent practice of ministers today. We are a part of a great cloud of witnesses, benefiting from others and hopefully establishing an example of faithfulness for the future.

Tom J. Nettles
Louisville, KY

INTRODUCTION

There are some men in the pages of history, whose greatness no person of common sense thinks of disputing. They tower above the herd of mankind, like the Pyramids, the Parthenon, and the Colosseum, among buildings. Such men were Luther and Augustine, Gustavus Adolphus and George Washington, Columbus and Sir Isaac Newton. He who questions their greatness must be content to be thought very ignorant, very prejudiced, or very eccentric. Public opinion has come to a conclusion about them—they were great men.

But there are also great men whose reputation lies buried under a heap of cotemporary ill-will and misrepresentation. The world does not appreciate them, because the world does not know their real worth. Their characters have come down to us through poisoned channels. Their portraits have been drawn by the ill-natured hand of enemies. Their faults have been exaggerated. Their excellences have been maliciously kept back and suppressed. Like the famous sculptures of Nineveh, they need the hand of some literary Layard to clear away the rubbish that has accumulated round their names, and show them to the world in their fair proportions. Such men were Vigilantius and Wycliffe.[5] Such men were Oliver Cromwell and many of the Puritans. And such a man was George Whitefield.

There are few men whose characters have suffered so much from ignorance and misrepresentation of the truth as Whitefield's.

That he was a famous Methodist, and ally of John Wesley, in the last century; that he was much run after by ignorant people, for his preaching; that many thought him an enthusiast and fanatic; all this is about as much as most Englishmen know.

But that he was one of the principal champions of evangelical religion in the eighteenth century in our own country; that he was one of the most powerful and effective preachers that ever lived; that he was a man of extraordinary singleness of eye, and devotedness to the interests of true religion; that he was a regularly ordained clergyman of the Church of England, and would always have worked in the Church, if the Church had not, most unwisely, shut him out; all these are things, of which few people seem aware. And yet, after calm

---

[5] Original: Wickliffe.

examination of his life and writings, I am satisfied this is the true account that ought to be given of George Whitefield.

My chief desire is to assist in forming a just estimate of Whitefield's worth. I wish to lend a helping hand toward raising his name from the undeservedly low place which is commonly assigned to it. I wish to place him before your eyes as a noble specimen of what the grace of God can enable one man to do. I want you to treasure up his name in your memories, as one of the brightest in that company of departed saints who were, in their day, patterns of good works, and of whom the world was not worthy.

I propose, therefore, without further preface, to give you a hasty sketch of Whitefield's times, Whitefield's life, Whitefield's religion, Whitefield's preaching, and Whitefield's actual work on earth.

1

WHITEFIELD'S TIMES

The story of Whitefield's times is one that should often be told. Without it nobody is qualified to form an opinion either as to the man or his acts. Conduct that in one kind of times may seem rash, extravagant, and indiscreet, in another may be wise, prudent, and even absolutely necessary. In forming your opinion of the comparative merits of Christian men, never forget the old rule, "Distinguish between times." Place yourself in each man's position. Do not judge what was a right course of action in other times, by what seems a right course of action in your own.

Now, the times when Whitefield lived were, unquestionably, the worst times that have ever been known in this country, since the Protestant Reformation. There never was a greater mistake than to talk of "the good old times." The times of the eighteenth century, at any rate, were "bad old times," unmistakably.

Whitefield was born in 1714. He died in 1770. It is not saying too much to assert, that this was precisely the darkest age that England has passed through in the last three hundred years. Anything more deplorable than the condition of the country, as to religion, morality, and high principal, from 1700 to about the era of the French Revolution, it is very difficult to conceive.

The state of religion in the Established Church[6] can only be compared to that of a frozen or palsied carcass. There were the time-honored formularies which the wisdom of the Reformers had provided. There were the services and lessons from Scripture, just in the same order as we have them now. But as to preaching the Gospel in the Established Church, there was almost none. The distinguishing doctrines of Christianity—the atonement, the work and office of Christ and the Spirit—were comparatively lost sight of. The vast majority of sermons were miserable moral essays, utterly devoid of anything calculated to awaken, convert, save or sanctify souls. The curse of black Bartholomew-day[7] seemed to rest upon our Church. For at least a century after casting out two thousand of the best ministers in England, our Establishment never prospered.

---

[6] *Established Church* is a reference to the Church of England.

[7] *Black Bartholomew Day* was August 24, 1662. Also known as *The Great Ejection.* When some 2,000 Protestant ministers were ejected from the Church of England for non-conformity. —C.H.

There were some learned and conscientious bishops at this era, beyond question. Such men were Secker, and Gibson, and Lowth, and Warburton, and Butler, and Horne. But even the best of them sadly misunderstood the requirements of the day they lived in. They spent their strength in writing apologies for Christianity, and contending against infidels. They could not see that, without the direct preaching of the essential doctrines of Christ's Gospel, their labors were all in vain. And, as to the majority of the bishops, they were potent for negative evil, but impotent for positive good; giants at stopping what they thought disorder, but infants at devising anything to promote real order; mighty to repress over-zealous attempts at evangelization, but weak to put in action any remedy for the evils of the age; eagle-eyed at detecting any unhappy wight[8] who trod on the toes of a rubric or canon, but blind as bats to the flood of indolence and false doctrine with which their dioceses were everywhere deluged.

That there were many well-read, respectable and honorable men among the parochial clergy at this period, it would be wrong to deny. But few, it is to be feared, out of the whole number, preached Christ crucified in simplicity and sincerity. Many whose lives were decent and moral, were notoriously Arians, if not Socinians. Many were totally engrossed in secular pursuits; they

---

[8] *Wight* meaning a person of a specified kind, especially one regarded as unfortunate.

neither did good themselves, nor liked anyone else to do it for them. They hunted; they shot; they drank; they swore; they fiddled; they farmed; they toasted Church and King, and thought little or nothing about saving souls. And as for the man who dared to preach the doctrine of the Bible, the Articles, and the Homilies, he was sure to be set down as an enthusiast and fanatic.

The state of religion among the Dissenters was only a few degrees better than the state of the Church. The toleration which they enjoyed from William the Third's time[9] was certainly productive of a very bad spiritual effect on them as a body. As soon as they ceased to be persecuted, they appear to have gone to sleep. The Baptist and Independent could still point to Gill, and Guyse, and Doddridge, and Watts, and a few more like-minded men. But the English Presbyterians were fast lapsing into Socinianism. And as to the great majority of nonconformists, it is vain to deny that they were very different men from Baxter,[10] and Flavel, and Gurnall, and Traill. A generation of preachers arose who were very orthodox, but painfully cold; very conscientious, but very wanting in spirituality; very constant in their objections to the Established Church, but very careless about spreading vital Christianity.

I deeply feel the difficulty of conveying a correct impression of the times when Whitefield lived. I dislike

---

[9] William III (1650–1702), was king of England, Ireland and Scotland from 1698 to 1702.

[10] See J. C. Ryle, *Baxter* (Peterborough: H&E Publishing, 2018).

over-statement as much as anyone, but I am thoroughly persuaded it is not easy to make an over-statement on this branch of my subject.

These were the times when the highest personages in the realm lived openly in ways which were flatly contrary to the law of God, and no man rebuked them. No courts, I suppose, can be imagined more diametrically unlike than the courts of George I and George II, and the court of Queen Victoria.

These were the times when reckless extravagance[11] and irreligion were reputable and respectable things. Judging from the description we have of men and manners in those days, a gentle man might have been defined as a creature who got drunk, gambled, swore, fought duels, and broke the seventh commandment incessantly. And for all this no one thought the worst of him.

These were the days when the men whom kings delighted to honor were Bolingbroke, Chesterfield, Walpole, and Newcastle. To be an infidel or a skeptic, to obtain power by intrigue, and to retain power by the grossest and most notorious bribery, were considered no disqualifications at this era. Such was the utter want of religion, morality, and high principle in the land, that men such as these were not only tolerated, but praised.

These were the days when Hume, the historian, put forth his work, became famous, and got a pension. He

---

[11] Original: when profligacy and.

was notoriously an infidel. These were the days when Sterne and Swift wrote their clever, but most indecent productions. Both were clergymen, and high in the Church; but the public saw no harm. These were the days when Fielding and Smollet were the popular authors, and the literary taste of high and low was suited by Roderick Random, Peregrine Pickle, Joseph Andrews, and Tom Jones. These were the days when Knox says, in his history of Christian Philosophy:

> Some of the most learned men—the most voluminous writers on theological subjects— were totally ignorant of Christianity. They were ingenious heathen philosophers, assuming the name of Christians, and forcibly paganizing Christianity, for the sake of pleasing the world.[12]

These were the days when Archbishop Drummond (1760) could talk of intricate and senseless questions, about the influence of the Spirit and power of grace, predestination, imputed righteousness, justification without works, and other opinions which have from the beginning, perplexed and perverted, debased, defiled, and wounded Christianity. These were the days when Bishop Warburton considered the teaching office of the Holy Spirit[13] to be completed in the Holy Scripture, and

---

[12] Vicemus Knox, *Christian Philosophy*, (London: Walton and Maberly, 1854), 269.

[13] Original: Holy Ghost.

that his sanctifying and comforting offices are chiefly confined to charity. Such were the leading ministers. What must the mass of teachers have been! Such were the priests of Whitefield's time. What must have been the people!

These were the days when there was an utter lack of sound theological writing. The doctrines of the Reformers were trampled under-foot by men who occupied their chairs. The bread of the Church was eaten by men who flatly contradicted her Articles. The appetite of religious people was satisfied with *Tillotson's Sermons,* and the *Whole Duty of Man.* A pension of two hundred pounds a year was actually given to Blair, of Edinburgh, for writing his most unchristian sermons. Ask any theological bookseller, and he will tell you that, generally speaking, no divinity is so worthless as that of the eighteenth century.

Finally,[14] these were the days when there was no Society for promoting the increase of true religion, but the Christian Knowledge Society, and the Society for the Propagation of the Gospel. And even their work was comparatively trifling. Nothing was done for the Jew. Nothing was done for the heathen. Nothing, almost, was done for the colonies. Nothing was done for the destitute part of our own country. Nothing was done for education. The Church slept. The dissenters slept. The pulpit slept. The religious press slept. The gates were left wide open.

---

[14] Original: In fine.

The walls were left unguarded. Infidelity stalked in. The Devil sowed tares extensively,[15] and walked to and fro. The gentry[16] gloried in their shame, and no man pointed out their wickedness. The people sinned with a high hand, and no man taught them better. Ignorance, profligacy, irreligion, and superstition were to be seen everywhere. Such were the times when Whitefield was raised up.

I know that this is a dreadful picture. I marvel God did not sweep away the Church altogether. But I believe that the picture is not one too highly coloured. It is painful to expose such a state of things. But, for Whitefield's sake, the truth ought to be known. Justice has not been done to him, because the condition of the times he lived in is not considered. The times he lived in were extraordinary times, and required extraordinary means to be used. And whatever quiet men, sitting by their fireside in our day, may say to the contrary, I am satisfied that Whitefield was just the man for his times.

---

[15] Original: tares broadcast.

[16] *Gentry* being a well-off societal class of land owners.

2

WHITEFIELD'S LIFE

The story of Whitefield's life, which forms the next part of our subject, is one that is soon told. The facts and incidents of that life are few and simple, and I shall not dwell upon them at any length.

Early life

Whitefield was born in 1714. Like many other great men, he was of very humble origin. His father and mother kept the Bell Inn, in the city of Gloucester.

Whitefield's early life seems to have been anything but religious, though he had occasional fits of devout feeling. He speaks of himself as having been addicted to lying, filthy talking and foolish joking.[17] He confesses that he was a Sabbath-breaker, a theater-goer, a card-

---

[17] Original: foolish jesting.

player, and a romance-reader. All this went on till he was twelve or fifteen years old.

At the age of twelve[18] he was placed at a grammar-school in Gloucester. Little is known of his progress there, except the curious fact that even then he was remarkable for his good articulation[19] and memory, and was selected to make speeches before the corporation, at their annual visitations.

At the age of fifteen[20] he appears to have become tired of Latin and Greek, and to have given up all hopes of ever becoming more than a tradesman. He ceased to take lessons in anything but writing. He began to assist his mother in the public-house that she kept. "At length," he says, "I put on my blue apron, washed mops, cleaned rooms, and, in one word, became a professed common drawer for near a year and a half."[21]

But God, who orders all things in heaven and earth, and called David from keeping sheep to be a king, had provided some better thing for Whitefield than the office of a potboy.[22] Family disagreements interfered with his prospects at the Bell Inn. An old school-fellow stirred up again within him the desire of going to the University.

---

[18] 1726.

[19] Original: good elocution.

[20] 1729.

[21] Robert Philip, *The Life and Times of the Reverend George Whitefield* (London: George Virtue, Bungay: J.R and C.Childs, 1837), 7.

[22] *Potboy* being a boy or man who worked at a pubic house to collect empty pots or glasses.

And at length, after several providential circumstances had smoothed the way, he was launched, at the age of eighteen,[23] at Oxford, in a position at that time much more humbling than it is now, as a servitor[24] at Pembroke College.

Whitefield's Oxford career seems to have been the turning-point in his life. According to his own journal, he had not been without religious convictions for two or three years before he went to Oxford. From the time of his entering Pembroke College, these convictions rapidly ripened into decided Christianity. He became marked for his attendance on all means of grace within his reach. He spent his leisure time in visiting the city prisons and doing good. He formed an acquaintance with the famous John Wesley and his brother Charles, which gave a colour to the whole of his subsequent life. At one time, he seems to have had a narrow escape from becoming a semi-Papist, an ascetic, or a mystic. From this he seems to have been delivered, partly by the advice of wiser and more experienced Christians, and partly by reading such books as Scougal's *Life of God in the Soul of Man*,[25] Law's

---

[23] 1732.

[24] *Servitor* being a student who would work as a servant in exchange for financial costs of the institution being covered.

[25] Henry Scougal, *The life of God in the soul of man. Or, The nature and excellency of the Christian religion; with the method of attaining the happiness it proposes. And an account of the beginning and advances of a spiritual life. In two letters written to persons of honour, with a preface by Gilbert Burnet* (London 1677).

Serious Call,[26] Baxter's *Call to the Unconverted,*[27] and Alleine's *Alarm to Unconverted Sinners.*[28] At length, in 1736, at the early age of twenty-two, he was ordained deacon by Bishop Benson, of Gloucester, and began to run that ministerial race in which he never drew breath till he was laid in the grave.

His first sermon was preached in St. Mary-le-Crypt, Gloucester. It was said to have driven fifteen persons mad. Bishop Benson remarked, that he only hoped the madness might continue. He next accepted temporary duty at the Tower Chapel, London. While engaged there, he preached continually in many of the London churches, and among others, in the parish churches of Islington, Bishopsgate, St. Dunstan's, St. Margaret, Westminster, and Bow, Cheapside. From the very beginning he attained a degree of popularity such as no preacher, probably, before or since, has ever reached. To say that the churches were crowded when he preached, would be saying little. They were literally crammed to suffocation. An eye-witness said, "You might have walked on the people's heads."

---

[26] William Law, *A Serious Call to a Devout and Holy Life* (London: William Innys, 1729).

[27] Richard Baxter, *A Call to the Unconverted, to Turn and Live: And Accept of Mercy, While Mercy May be Had: as Ever They Will Find Mercy, in the Day of Their Extremity, from the Living God* (York: Wilson, Spence, and Mawman, 1791).

[28] Joseph Alleine, *An Alarm to unconverted sinners* (London: Tho. Parkhurst at the Bible and Three Crowns, 1691).

From London he removed for a few months to Dummer, a little rural parish in Hampshire, near Basingstoke. From Dummer he sailed for the colony of Georgia, in North America, after visiting Gloucester and Bristol, and preaching in crowded churches in each place. The object of his voyage was to assist the Wesleys in the care of an Orphan House which they had established in Georgia for the children of colonists who died there. The management of this Orphan House ultimately devolved entirely on Whitefield, and entailed on him a world of responsibility and anxiety all his life long. Though well meant, it seems to have been a design of very questionable wisdom.

Whitefield returned from Georgia after about two years' absence, partly to obtain priest's orders, which were conferred on him by Bishop Benson, and partly on business connected with the Orphan House. And now we reach the era in his life when he was obliged, by circumstances, to take up a line of conduct as a minister which he probably at one time never contemplated, but which was made absolutely necessary by the treatment he received.

Whitefield as an open-air preacher
It appears that on arriving in London after his first visit to Georgia, he found the countenances of many of the clergy no longer toward him as they were before. They had taken fright at some expressions in his published letters, and some reports of his conduct in America.

They were scandalized at his preaching the doctrine of regeneration in the way that he did, as a thing which many of their parishioners needed. The pulpits of many churches were flatly refused to him. Chuchwardens, who had no eyes for heresy and drunkenness, were filled with virtuous indignation about what they called breaches of order. Bishops who could tolerate Arianism and Socinianism, got into a state of excitement about a man who simply preached the Gospel, and put forth warnings against fanaticism and enthusiasm. In short, Whitefield's field of usefulness within the Church was rapidly narrowed on every side.

The step which seems to have decided Whitefield's course of action at this period of his life, was his adoption of open-air preaching. He had gone to Islington, on a Sunday in April, 1739, to preach for the vicar, his friend, Mr. Stonehouse. In the midst of the prayers, the churchwarden came to him, and demanded his license for preaching in the London diocese. This Whitefield, of course, had not got, any more than any clergyman not regularly officiating in the diocese has at this day. The upshot of the matter was, that being forbidden to preach in the pulpit, he went outside, after the service, and preached in the churchyard. From that day he regularly took up the practice of open-air preaching. Wherever there were large open fields around London; where ever there were large bands of idle, church despising, Sabbath-breaking people gathered together—there went Whitefield and lifted up his voice. The Gospel so proclaimed was listened to, and greedily received by hundreds who had never dreamed of visiting a place of worship. In Moorfields, in Hackney Fields, in Mary-le-bone Fields, in May Fair, in Smithfield, on Kennington Common, on Blackheath, Sunday after Sunday, Whitefield preached to admiring masses. Ten thousand, fifteen thousand, twenty thousand, thirty thousand, were computed sometimes to have heard him at once. The cause of pure religion, beyond doubt, was advanced. Souls were plucked from the hand of Satan, as brands from the burning. But it was going much too fast for the Church of those days. The clergy, with very few exceptions, would have nothing to do with this strange preacher. In short, the ministrations of Whitefield in the pulpits of the Establishment, with an occasional exception, from this time ceased. He loved the Church. He gloried in her Articles and Formularies. He used her Prayer Book with delight. But the Church did not love him, and so lost the use of his services. The plain truth is, the Church of England of that day was not ready for a man like Whitefield. The Church was too much asleep to understand him.

From this date to the day of his death, a period of thirty-one years, Whitefield's life was one uniform employment. From Sunday morning to Saturday night— from the 1st of January to the 31st of December—except when laid aside by illness, he was almost incessantly preaching. There was hardly a considerable town in England, Scotland, and Wales, that he did not visit.

When churches were opened to him, he gladly preached in churches. When chapels were only offered, he cheerfully preached in chapels. When church and chapel alike were closed, he was ready and willing to preach in the open air. For thirty-four years he labored in this way, always proclaiming the same glorious Gospel, and always, as far as man's eye can judge, with immense effect. In one single Whitsuntide week, after he had been preaching at Moor-fields, he received one thousand letters from people under spiritual concern, and admitted to the Lord's table three hundred and fifty persons. In the thirty-four years of his ministry, it is reckoned that he preached publicly eighteen thousand times.

Whitefield's journeyings

His journeyings were tremendous,[29] when the roads and conveyances of his times are considered. Fourteen times he visited Scotland. Seven times he crossed the Atlantic, backward and forward. Twice he went over to Ireland. As to England and Wales, he traversed every county in them, from the Isle of Wight to Berwick-on-Tweed, and from the Land's End to the North Foreland.

His regular ministerial work in London, when he was not journeying, was prodigious. His weekly engagements at the Tabernacle in Tottenham-court Road, which was built for him when the pulpits of the

---

[29] Original: were prodigious.

Established Church were closed, were as follows: Every Sunday morning he administered the Lord's Supper to several hundred communicants, at half-past six. After this he read prayers, and preached, both morning and afternoon; preached again in the evening at half-past five; and concluded, by addressing a large society of widows, married people, young men and spinsters, all sitting separately in the area of the Tabernacle, with exhortations suitable to their respective stations. On Monday, Tuesday, Wednesday, and Thursday mornings, he preached regularly at six. On Monday, Tuesday, Wednesday, Thursday and Saturday evenings, he delivered lectures. This you will observe made thirteen sermons a week. And all this time he was carrying on a correspondence with people in almost every part of the world.

That any human frame could so long endure the labor he went through, does indeed seem wonderful. That his life was not shortened by violence, is no less wonderful. Once he was nearly stoned to death by a Popish mob in Dublin. Once he was nearly murdered in bed by an angry lieutenant of the navy at Plymouth. Once he narrowly escaped being stabbed by the sword of a rakish young gentleman in Moorfields; but he was immortal till his work was done. He died at last at Newburyport, in North America, from a fit of asthma, at the age of fifty-six. His last sermon was preached only twenty-four hours before his death. It was an open-air discourse two hours long. Like Bishop Jewell, he almost

21

died preaching. He left no children. He was once married, and the marriage does not seem to have contributed much to his happiness. But he left a name far better than that of sons and daughters. Never, I believe, was there a man of whom it could be so truly said, that he spent and was spent for God.

3

WHITEFIELD'S RELIGION

The story of Whitefield's religion is the next part of the subject that I proposed to take up, and unquestionably it is one of no little interest.

Doctrine

What sort of doctrine did this wonderful man preach? What were the standards of faith to which he adhered under the Bible? What were the peculiar essentials of this religious teaching of his, which was so universally spoken against in his day?

The answer to all these questions is short and simple. Whitefield was a real, genuine son of the Church of England. As such he was brought up in early youth. As such he was educated at Oxford. As such he preached as long as he was allowed to preach within the Establishment. As such he preached when he was outside. References to the Prayer Book, Articles, and Homilies, abound in all his writings and sermons. His constant reply to his numerous opponents was, that he at any rate was consistent with the formularies of his own Church, and that they were not. It is not at all too much to say, that when practically cast out of the Establishment, Whitefield was an infinitely better churchman than ten thousand of the men who received the tithes of the Church of England, and remained comfortably behind.

Whitefield no doubt was not a churchman of the stamp of Archbishop Laud and his school. He was not the man to put a Romish interpretation on our excellent Formularies, and to place Church and sacraments before Christ. He was not a churchman of the stamp of Tillotson and the school that followed him. He did not lay aside justification by faith, and the need of grace, for semi-heathen disquisitions about morality and duty, virtue and vice. And he was quite right. Laud and his followers went infinitely beyond the doctrines of our Church. Tillotson and his school fell infinitely below.

But if a churchman is a man who reads the Articles, and Liturgy, and Homilies, in the sense of the men who compiled them—if a churchman is a man who sympathizes with Cranmer, and Latimer, and Hooper, and Jewell—if a churchman is a man who honors doctrines and ordinances in the order and proportion that the Thirty-nine Articles honor them—if this be the true definition of a church man, then Whitefield was the

highest style of churchman—as true a churchman as
ever breathed. And as for Whitefield's adversaries, they
were little better than shams and impostors. They had
place and power on their side, but they scarcely deserve
to be called church men at all.

Perhaps no better test of Whitefield's religious
opinions can be supplied, than the list of authors in
divinity which he wrote out for the use of a college
connected with his Orphan House in Georgia. Of
churchmen, this list includes the names of Archbishop
Leighton, Bishop Hall, and Burkitt; of Puritans, Pool,
Owen, and Bunyan; of Dissenters, Matthew Henry and
Doddridge; of Scotch Presbyterians, Wilson and Boston.
All these are men whose praise is even now in all the
churches. These, let us understand, were the kind of
men with whom he was of one mind in doctrine.

Theological teaching
As to the substance of Whitefield's theological teaching,
the simplest account I can give of it is, that it was purely
evangelical. There were four main things that he never
lost sight of in his sermons. These four were: man's
complete ruin by sin, and consequent natural corruption
of heart; man's complete redemption by Christ, and
complete justification before God by faith in Christ;
man's need of regeneration by the Spirit, and entire
renewal of heart and life; and man's utter want of any
title to be considered a living Christian, unless he is dead
to sin and lives a holy life.

Whitefield had no notion of flattering men, and speaking smooth things to them, merely because they were baptized and called Christians, and sometimes came to church. He only looked at one prominent feature in the thousands he saw around him; and that was, the general character of their lives. He saw the lives of these multitudes were utterly contradictory to the Bible, and utterly at variance with the principles of the Church to which they professed to belong. He waited for nothing more. He looked for no further evidence. He judged of trees by their fruits. He told these thousands at once that they were in danger of being lost forever—that they were in the broad way that leads to destruction[30]— that they were dead, and must be made alive again[31]— that they were lost, and must be found.[32] He told them that if they loved life, they must immediately repent— they must become new creatures—they must be converted, they must be born again.[33] And I believe the apostles would have done just the same.

But Whitefield was just as full and explicit in setting forth the way to heaven as he was in setting forth the way to hell. When he saw that men's consciences were pricked and their fears aroused, he would open the treasure-house of gospel mercy, and spread forth before a congregation its unsearchable stores. He would unfold

---

[30] Matthew 7:13–14.
[31] Ephesians 2:1–10.
[32] Luke 15:1–7.
[33] John 3:3.

to them the amazing love of God the Father to a fallen world—that love from which he gave his only-begotten Son,[34] and on account of which, while we were yet sinners, Christ died for us.[35] He would show them the amazing love of God the Son in taking our nature on him, and suffering for us, the just for the unjust.[36] He would tell them of Jesus able to save to the uttermost all that would come to God by him—Jesus and his everlasting righteousness, in which the vilest sinner might stand complete and perfect before the throne of God—Jesus and the blood of sprinkling, which could wash the blackest sins away—Jesus the High Priest, waiting to receive all who would come to him, and not only mighty, but ready to save. And all this glorious salvation, he would tell men, was close to them. It was not far above them, like heaven. It was not deep beneath them, like hell. It was near at hand. It was within their reach. He would urge them at once to accept it. The man that felt his sins and desired deliverance had only to believe and be saved, to ask and receive, to wash and be clean. And was he not right to say so? I believe the apostles would have said much the same.

But while Whitefield addressed the careless and ungodly masses in this style, he never failed to urge on those who made a high profession of religion their responsibility, and to stir them up to walk worthy of their

---

[34] John 3:16.
[35] Romans 5:8.
[36] 1 Peter 3:18.

high calling. He never tolerated men who talked well about religion, but lived inconsistent lives. Such men, no doubt, there were about him, but it is pretty certain they got no quarter from him. On the contrary, one of his biographers tells us that he was especially careful to impress upon all the members of his congregation the absolute necessity of adorning the doctrine of God in all the relations of life. Masters and servants, rich people and poor, old and young, married and single, each and all were plainly exhorted to glorify God in their respective positions. One day he would tell the young men of his congregation to beware of being like one he heard of, whose uncle described him as such a jumble of religion and business, that he was fit for neither. Another day he would hold up the example of a widow, remarkable for her confidence in God. Another day he would say to them, "God convert you more and more every hour of the day; God convert you from lying in bed in the morning; God convert you from lukewarmness; God convert you from conformity to the world!" Another day he would warn young men against leaving their religion behind them as they rose in the world. "Beware," he would say, "of being golden apprentices, silver journeymen, and copper masters." In short, there never was a greater mistake than to suppose there was anything antinomian or licentious in Whitefield's teaching. It was discriminating, unquestionably. Sinners had their portion; but saints had their portion too. And what was this but walking in the very steps of the apostle Paul?

The crowning excellence of Whitefield's teaching was, that he just spoke of men, things, and doctrines, in the way that the Bible speaks of them, and the place that the Bible assigns to them. God, Christ, and the Spirit—sin, justification, conversion, and sanctification—impenitent sinners the most miserable of people—believing saints the most privileged of people—the world a vain and empty thing—heaven the only rest for an immortal soul—the Devil a tremendous and ever-watchful foe—holiness the only true happiness—hell a real and certain portion for the unconverted; these were the kind of subjects which filled Whitefield's mind, and formed the staple of his ministry. To say that he undervalued the sacraments would be simply false. His weekly communions at the Tabernacle are an answer that speaks for itself. But he never put the first things in Christianity second, and the second first. He never put doctrines below sacraments, and sacraments above doctrine. And who shall dare to blame him for this? He only followed the proportion of the Bible.

Whitefield practiced what he preached

It is only fair to add, that Whitefield exemplified in his practice the religion that he preached. He had faults, unquestionably. I write not in order[37] to make him out a

---

[37] Original: I have not come here to make.

perfect being. He often erred in judgment. He was often hasty, both with his tongue and with his pen. He had no business to say that Archbishop Tillotson knew no more of religion than Mohammed. He was wrong to set down some people as the Lord's enemies, and others as the Lord's friends, so precipitately as he sometimes did. He was to blame for styling many of the clergy letter-learned Pharisees, because they could not receive the doctrine of the new birth. But still, after all this has been said, here can be no doubt that, in the main he was a holy, self-denying, and consistent man. Even his worst enemies can say nothing to the contrary.

He was, to the very end, a man of *eminent self-denial.* His style of living was most simple. He refused money when it was pressed upon him, and once to the amount of seven thousand pounds. He amassed no fortune. He founded no wealthy family. The little money he left behind him at his death was entirely from the legacies of friends.

He was a man of remarkable *disinterestedness* and singleness of eye. He seemed to live for only two objects—the glory of God, and the salvation of immortal souls. He raised no party of followers who took his name. He established no system, like Wesley, of which his own writings should be cardinal elements. A frequent expression of his is most characteristic of the man: "Let the name of George Whitefield perish, so long as Christ only is exalted."

Last, but not least, he was a man of *extraordinary catholicity and liberality* in his religion. He knew nothing of that narrow-minded policy which prompts a man to fancy that everything must be barren outside his own camp, and that his party has got a monopoly of truth and heaven. He loved all who loved the Lord Jesus Christ in sincerity. He measured all by the measure which the angels of God use—"did they possess repentance toward God, faith toward the Lord Jesus Christ, holiness of conversation?" If they did, they were as his brethren. His soul was with such men, by whatever name they were called. Minor differences were wood, hay, and stubble to him. The marks of the Lord Jesus were the only marks he cared for. This catholicity is the more remarkable, when the spirit of the times he lived in is considered. Even the Erskines, in Scotland, wanted him to preach for no other denomination but their own, namely, the Secession Church. He asked them, why only for them; and received the notable answer, that they were the Lord's people. This was more than Whitefield could stand. He asked if there were no other Lord's people but themselves. He told them, if all others were the Devil's people, they certainly had more need to be preached to. And he wound up by informing them, that if the Pope himself would lend him his pulpit, he would gladly proclaim the righteousness of Christ in it. To this catholicity of spirit he adhered all his days. And nothing could be a more weighty testimony against all narrowness of spirit among believers, than his request, shortly before his death, that when he did die, John Wesley might be asked to preach his funeral sermon. Wesley and he had long ceased to see eye to eye on Calvinistic points. But as Calvin said of Luther, so Whitefield was resolved to think of Wesley. He was determined to sink minor differences, and to know him only as a good servant of Jesus Christ.

Such was George Whitefield's religion. Comment, I hope, is needless upon it. Time, at any rate, forbids me to dwell on it a moment longer. But surely I think I have shown enough to justify me in expressing a wish that we had many living ministers in the Church of England like George Whitefield.

4

WHITEFIELD'S PREACHING

The next part of the subject is one which I feel some difficulty in handling—I allude to Whitefield's preaching.

I find that this point is one on which much difference of opinion prevails. I find many are disposed to think that part of Whitefield's success is attributable to the novelty of Gospel doctrines at the times when he preached, and part to the extraordinary gifts of voice and delivery with which he was endowed, and that the matter and style of his sermons were in no wise remarkable. From this opinion I am inclined to dissent altogether. After calm examination, I have come to the conclusion that Whitefield was one of the most powerful and extraordinary preachers the world has ever seen. My belief is, that until now[38] he has never been too highly

---

[38] Original: hitherto.

estimated, and that, on the contrary, he does not receive the credit he deserves.

Whitefield's effectiveness

One thing is abundantly clear and beyond dispute, and that is, that his sermons were wonderfully effective. No preacher has ever succeeded in arresting the attention of such enormous crowds of people as those he addressed continually in the neighborhood of London. No preacher has ever been so universally popular in every country he visited, England, Scotland, and America, as he was. No preacher has ever retained his hold on his hearers so entirely as he did for thirty-four years. His popularity never waned. It was as great at the end of his days as it was at the beginning. This of itself is a great fact. To command the ear of people for thirty-four long years, and be preaching incessantly the whole time, is something that the novelty of the Gospel alone will not account for. The theory that his preaching was popular, because new, to my mind is utterly unsatisfactory.

Another thing is no less indisputable about his preaching, and that is, that it produced a powerful effect on people in every rank of life. He won the suffrages of high as well as low, of rich as well as poor, of learned as well as unlearned. If his preaching had been popular with none but the uneducated masses, we might have thought it possible there was little in it except a striking delivery and a loud voice. But facts are, unfortunately, against this theory too; and, under the pressure of these facts, it will be found to break down.

It is a fact, that numbers of the nobility and gentry of Whitefield's day were warm admirers of his preaching. The Marquis of Lothian, the Earl of Leven, the Earl of Buchan, Lord Rae, Lord Dartmouth, Lord James A. Gordon, might be named, among others, besides Lady Huntingdon, and a host of ladies.

It is a fact, that eminent statesmen, like Bolingbroke and Chesterfield, were frequently his delighted hearers. Even the artificial Chesterfield was known to warm under Whitefield's eloquence. Bolingbroke has placed on record his opinion, and said, "He is the most extraordinary man in our times. He has the most commanding eloquence I ever heard in any person."

It is a fact, that cool-headed men, like Hume the historian, and Franklin the philosopher, spoke in no measured terms of his preaching powers. Franklin has written a long account of the effect his sermons produced at Philadelphia. Hume declared that it was worth going twenty miles to hear him.

Now these are facts—simple, historical, and well-authenticated facts. What shall we say to them? I say that these facts are quite enough to prove that Whitefield's effectiveness was not owing entirely to delivery and voice, as some men would have us believe. Bolingbroke and Chesterfield, and Hume, and Franklin, were not such weak men as to allow their judgments to be biased by any mere external endowments. They were no mean judges of eloquence. They were, probably, among the best qualified critics of the day. And I say confidently, that their opinion can only be explained by the fact, that Whitefield was indeed a most powerful and extraordinary preacher.

But still, after all, the question remains to be answered: What was the secret of Whitefield's unparalleled success as a preacher? How are we to account for his sermons producing effects which no sermons, before or after his time, have ever yet done? These are questions you have a right to ask. But they are questions I find it very hard to answer. That his sermons were not mere voice and rant, I think, we have pretty clearly proved. That he was a man of commanding intellect, and grasp of mind, no one has ever pretended to say. How then are we to account for the effectiveness of his preaching?

The reader who turns for a solution of this question to the seventy-five sermons published under his name, will probably be much disappointed. He will not find in them many striking thoughts. He will not discover in them any new exhibitions of Gospel doctrine. The plain truth is, that by far the greater part of them were taken down in shorthand by reporters, without Whitefield's knowledge, and published without correction. No intelligent reader, I think, can help discovering that these reporters were, must unhappily, ignorant alike of stopping and paragraphing, of grammar, and of Gospel. The consequence is, that many passages in these sermons are what Latimer[39] would call a "mingle-mangle," or what we should call in this day "a complete mess."

Nevertheless, I am bold to say, that with all their faults, Whitefield's printed sermons will repay a candid perusal. Let the reader only remember what I have just said, that most of them are miserably reported, paragraphed, and stopped, and make allowance accordingly. Let him remember, also, that English for speaking and English for reading are two different languages; and that sermons which preach well, always read ill. Remember these two things, I say, and I do believe you will find very much to admire in some of Whitefield's sermons. For myself, I can only say, I believe I have learned much from them, and however great a heresy against taste it may appear, I should be ungrateful if I did not praise them.

Characteristic features of Whitefield's sermons

And now let me try to point out to you what seem to me to have been the characteristic features of Whitefield's sermons. I may be wrong, but they appear to me to present just such a combination of excellences as is most likely to make an effective preacher.

---

[39] See J.C. Ryle, *Latimer* (Peterborough: H&E Publishing, 2018).

A pure gospel

First and foremost, you must remember, Whitefield preached a singularly pure Gospel. Few men ever gave their hearers so much wheat and so little chaff. He did not get into his pulpit to talk about his party, his cause, his interest, or his office. He was perpetually telling you about your sins, your heart, and Jesus Christ, in the way that the Bible speaks of them. "Oh! the righteousness of Jesus Christ!" he would frequently say: "I must be excused if I mention it in almost all my sermons." This, you may be sure, is the cornerstone of all preaching that God honors. It must be pre-eminently a manifestation of truth.

Lucid and simple

For another thing, Whitefield's preaching was singularly lucid and simple. You might not like his doctrine, perhaps; but at any rate you could not fail to understand what he meant. His style was easy, plain, and conversational. He seemed to abhor long and involved sentences. He always saw his mark, and went direct at it. He seldom or never troubled his hearers with long arguments and intricate reasonings. Simple Bible statements, pertinent anecdotes, and apt illustrations, were the more common weapons that he used. The consequence was, that his hearers always understood him. He never shot above their heads. Never did man seem to enter so thoroughly into the wisdom of Archbishop Usher's saying, "To make easy things seem hard is easy, but to make hard things easy is the office of a great preacher."

Bold and direct

For another thing, Whitefield was a singularly bold and direct preacher. He never used that indefinite expression, "we," which seems so peculiar to English pulpit oratory, and which leaves a hearer's mind in a state of misty confusion as to the preacher's meaning. He met men face to face, like one who had a message from God to them—like an ambassador with tidings from heaven; "I have come here to speak to you about your soul." He never minced matters, and beat about the bush in attacking prevailing sins. His great object seemed to be to discover the dangers his hearers were most liable to, and then fire right at their hearts. The result was, that hundreds of his hearers used always to think that the sermons were specially addressed to themselves. He was not content, like many, with sticking on a tailpiece of application at the end of a long discourse. A constant vein of application run through all his sermons. "This is for you: this is for you: and this is for you." His hearers were never let alone. Nothing, however, was more striking than his direct appeals to all classes of his congregation, as he drew toward a conclusion. With all the faults of his printed sermons, the conclusions of some of them are, to my mind, the most stirring and heart-searching addresses to souls that are to be found in the English language.

Earnest

Another striking feature in Whitefield's preaching was his thundering earnestness. One poor, uneducated man said of him, that he "preached like a lion." Never, perhaps, did any preacher so thoroughly succeed in showing people that he, at least, believed in all he was saying, and that his whole heart, and soul, and strength, were bent on making them believe it too. No man could say that his sermons were like the morning and evening gun at Portsmouth, a formal discharge, fired off as a matter of course, that disturbs nobody. They were all life. They were all fire. There was no getting away from under them. Sleep was next to impossible. You must listen whether you liked it or not. There was a holy violence about him. Your attention was taken by storm. You were fairly carried off your legs by his energy, before you had time to consider what you would do.

An American gentleman once went to hear him, for the first time, in consequence of the report he heard of his preaching powers. The day was rainy, the congregation comparatively thin, and the beginning of the sermon rather heavy. Our American friend began to say to himself, "This man is no great wonder after all." He looked round, and saw the congregation as little interested as himself. One old man, in front of the pulpit, had fallen asleep. But all at once Whitefield stopped short. His countenance changed. And then he suddenly broke forth in an altered tone: "If I had come to speak to you in my own name, you might well rest your elbows on

your knees, and your heads on your hands, and sleep;
and once in a while look up and say, 'What is this
babbler talking of?' But I have not come to you in my
own name. No! I have come to you in the name of the
Lord of Hosts," (here he brought down his hand and
foot with a forte that made the building ring,) "and I
must and will be heard." The congregation started. The
old man woke up at once. "Ay, ay!" cried Whitefield,
fixing his eyes on him, "I have waked you up, have I? I
meant to do it. I am not come here to preach to stocks
and stones: I have come to you in the name of the Lord
God of Hosts, and I must and will have an audience."
The hearers were stripped of their apathy at once. Every
word of the sermon was attended to. And the American
gentleman never forgot it.

Power of description

Another striking feature in Whitefield's preaching was
his singular power of description. The Arabians have a
proverb which says, "He is the best orator who can turn
men's ears into eyes." If ever there was a speaker who
succeeded in doing this, it was Whitefield. He drew such
vivid pictures of the things he was dwelling upon, that
his hearers could believe they actually saw them all with
their own eyes, and heard them with their own ears. "On
one occasion," says one of his biographers, "Lord
Chesterfield was among his hearers. The preacher, in
describing the miserable condition of a poor, benighted
sinner, illustrated the subject by describing a blind

beggar. The night was dark; the road dangerous and full of snares. The poor sightless mendicant is deserted by his dog near the edge of a precipice, and has nothing to grope his way with but his staff. But Whitefield so warmed with his subject, and unfolded it with such graphic power, that the whole auditory was kept in breathless silence over the movements of the poor old man;" and, at length, when the beggar was about to take that fatal step which would have hurled him down the precipice to certain destruction, Lord Chesterfield actually made a rush forward to save him, exclaiming aloud, "He is gone! He is gone!" The noble lord had been so entirely carried away by the preacher, that he forgot the whole was a picture.

Emotion

One more feature in Whitefield's preaching deserves especial notice, and that is, the immense amount of pathos[40] and feeling which it always contained. It was no uncommon thing with him to weep profusely in the pulpit. Cornelius Winter goes so far as to say that he hardly ever knew him get through a sermon without tears. There seems to have been nothing whatsoever of affectation in this. He felt intensely for the souls before him, and his feeling found a vent in tears. Of all the ingredients of his preaching, nothing, I suspect, was so powerful as this. It awakened sympathies, and touched

---

[40] *Pathos* meaning a quality that evokes pity or sadness.

secret springs in men, which no amount of intellect could have moved. It melted down the prejudices which many had conceived against him. They could not hate the man who wept so much over their souls. They were often so affected as to shed floods of tears themselves. "I came to hear you," said one man, "intending to break your head; but your sermon got the better of me—it broke my heart." Once you become satisfied that a man loves you, and you will listen gladly to anything he has got to say. And this was just one grand secret of Whitefield's success.

Action

And now I will only ask you to add to this feeble sketch, that Whitefield's action was perfect—so perfect that Garrick, the famous actor, gave it unqualified praise— that his voice was as wonderful as his action—so powerful, that he could make thirty thousand people hear him at once; so musical and well-attuned, that men said he could raise tears by his pronunciation of the word "Mesopotamia:" that his fluency and command of unplanned[41] language were of the highest order, prompting him always to use the right word and to put it in the right place. Add, I say, these gifts to those already mentioned, and then judge for yourselves whether there is not sufficient, and more than sufficient, in our hands, to account for his power as a preacher.

---

[41] Original: of extemporaneous language.

Conclusion

For my part, I say, unhesitatingly, that I believe no living preacher ever possessed such a combination of excellences as Whitefield. Some, no doubt, have surpassed him in some of his gifts; others, perhaps, have been his equals in others. But, for a combination of pure doctrine, simple and lucid style, boldness and directness, earnestness and fervor, descriptiveness and picture-drawing, pathos and feeling—united with a perfect voice, perfect delivery, and perfect command of words, Whitefield, I repeat, stands alone. No man, dead or alive, I believe, ever came alongside of him. And I believe you will always find, that just in proportion as preachers have approached that curious combination of excellences which Whitefield possessed, just in that very proportion have they attained what Clarendon defines true eloquence to be, namely, "a strange power of making themselves believed."

5

The Amount of Good Whitefield Did

And now, there only remains one more point connected with Whitefield to which I wish to show you.[42] I fear that I will have exhausted your attention already. But the point is one of such importance, that it cannot be passed over in silence. The point I mean is, the actual amount of real good that Whitefield did.

You will, I hope, understand me, when I say, that the materials for forming an opinion on this point in a history like his, must necessarily be limited.[43] He founded no denomination among whom his name was embalmed, and his every act recorded, as did John Wesley. He headed no mighty movement against a Church which openly professed false doctrines, as Luther did against Rome. He wrote no books which were

---

[42] Original: wish to advert.
[43] Original: must be scanty.

to be the religious classics of the million, like John Bunyan. He was a simple, unsophisticated[44] man, who lived for one thing only, and that was to preach Christ. If he succeeded in doing that effectually, he cared for nothing else. He did nothing to preserve the memory of his usefulness. He left his work with the Lord.

Of course, there are many people who can see in Whitefield nothing but a fanatic and enthusiast. There is a generation that loathes everything like zeal in religion. There are never lacking men of a cautious, cold-blooded, Erasmus-like temper, who pass through the world doing no good, because they are so dreadfully afraid of doing harm. I do not expect such men to admire Whitefield, or accept[45] he did any good. I fear, if they had lived in the first century,[46] they would have had no sympathy with St. Paul.

Again, there are other people who count division[47] a far greater crime than either heresy or false doctrine. There is a generation of men who under no circumstances will worship God out of their own parish: and as to separation from the Church, they seem to think that nothing whatsoever can justify it. I do not, of course, expect such men to admire Whitefield or his work. His principle evidently was, that it was far better for men to be uncanonically saved than canonically damned.

---

[44] Original: guileless man.
[45] Original: allow that he.
[46] Original: eighteen hundred years ago.
[47] Original: schism a far.

Whether by any other line of action Whitefield could have remained in the Church, and retained his usefulness, is a question which, at this distance of time, we are very incompetent to answer. That he erred in temper and judgment in his dealings with the bishops and clergy, in many instances, I have no doubt. That he raised up fresh bodies of separatists from the Church of England, and made breaches which probably will never be repaired, I have no doubt also. But still it must never be forgotten, that the state of the Church was bad enough to provoke a holy indignation. The old principle is most true, that "he is the schismatic who causes the separation, and not he who separates." If Whitefield did harm, the harm ought to be laid on the Church which compelled him to act as he did, quite as much as on him. And when we come to strike the balance, I believe the harm he may have done is outweighed by the good a thousand-fold.

The good that he did directly
The truth I believe is that the direct good Whitefield did to immortal souls was enormous. I will go further. I believe it is incalculable. In Scotland, in England, in America, credible witnesses have recorded their testimony that he was the means of converting thousands of souls.

Franklin, the philosopher, was a cold, calculating man, and not likely to speak too highly of any minister's work. Yet even he confessed that it "was wonderful to see the change soon made by his preaching in the manners of the inhabitants of Philadelphia. From being thoughtless or indifferent about religion, it seemed as if all the world were growing religious."

Maclaurin and Willison were Scotch ministers, whose names are well known to theological readers, and stand deservedly high. Both of them have testified that Whitefield did an amazing work in Scotland. Willison, in particular, says: "That God honored him with surprising success among sinners of all ranks and persuasions."

Old Venn, in our own Church, was a man of strong common sense, as well as great grace. His opinion was, that "if the greatness, extent, success, and disinterestedness of a man's labours can give him distinction among the children of Christ, then we are warranted to affirm, that scarce any has equaled Mr. Whitefield." Again, he says, "It is a well-known fact, that the conversion of men's souls has been the fruit of a single sermon from his lips, so eminently was he made a fisher of men." And again, "Though we are allowed to sorrow that we shall never see or hear him again, we must still rejoice that millions have heard him so long, so often, and to such good effect; and that out of this mass of people, multitudes are gone before him to hail his entrance into the world of glory."

John Newton was a shrewd man, as well as an eminent minister of the Gospel. His testimony is, "I am not backward to say, that I have not read or heard of any person, since the apostles' days, of whom it may more emphatically be said, he was a burning and a shining light, than the late Mr. Whitefield, whether we consider the warmth of his zeal, the greatness of his ministerial talents, or the extensive usefulness with which the Lord honored him."[48]

These are not solitary testimonies. I might add many more if time permitted. Romaine did not agree with him in many things, yet what does he say of him? "We have none left to succeed him; none, of his gifts; none, anything like him in usefulness." Toplady was a tremendous high Calvinist, and not disposed to overestimate the number of saved souls. Yet he says, Whitefield's ministry was "attended with spiritual benefit to tens of thousands;" and he styles him "the apostle of the British empire, and the prince of preachers." Hervey was a quiet, literary man, whose health seldom allowed him to quit the retirement of Weston Favell. But he says of Whitefield, "I never beheld so fair a copy of our Lord, such a living image of the Saviour. I cannot forbear applying the wise man's encomiums of an illustrious woman to this eminent minister of the everlasting Gospel: 'Many sons have done virtuously, but you excel them all.'"

---

[48] John Newton, *"He was a burning and shining light"* (A sermon on John 5:35, Olney, November 11, 1770).

Good that he did indirectly

But if the amount of direct good that Whitefield did in the world was great, who shall tell us the amount of good that he did indirectly? I believe it never can be reckoned up. I suspect it will never be fully known until the last day.

Stirred up a zeal for the Gospel

Whitefield was among the first who stirred up a zeal for the pure Gospel among the clergy and laity of our own Church. His constant assertion of pure Reformation principles—his repeated references to the Articles, Prayer Book, and Homilies—his never-answered challenges to his opponents to confute him out of the formularies of their own communion—all this must have produced an effect, and set many thinking. I have no doubt whatsoever, that many a faithful minister, who became a shining light in those days within the Church of England, first lighted his candle at the lamp of a man outside.

Showed the right way

Whitefield, again, was among the first to show the right way to meet infidels and skeptics. He saw clearly that the most powerful weapon against such men is not metaphysical reasoning and critical disquisition; but preaching the whole Gospel, living the whole Gospel, and spreading the whole Gospel. It was not the writings of Leland, and the younger Sherlock, and Waterland,

and Leslie, that rolled back the flood of infidelity one half so much as the preaching of Whitefield, and Wesley, and Fletcher, and Romaine, and Berridge, and Venn. Had it not been for them, I firmly believe we might have had a counterpart of the French Revolution in our own land. They were the men who were the true champions of Christianity. Infidels are seldom shaken by mere abstract reasoning. The surest arguments against them are Gospel truth and Gospel life.

Went after souls

To crown all, Whitefield was the very first who seems thoroughly to have understood what Chalmers has called the *aggressive system*. He did not wait for souls to come to him, but he went after souls. He did not sit tamely by his fireside, mourning over the wickedness of the land. He went forth to confront[49] the Devil in his high places. He attacked sin and wickedness face to face, and gave them no peace. He dived into holes and corners after sinners. He hunted up ignorance and vice wherever it could be found. He showed that he thoroughly realized the nature of the ministerial office. Like a fisherman, he did not wait for the fish to come to him. Like a fisherman, he used every kind of means to catch souls. Men know a little more of this now than they did formerly. City Missions, and District Visiting Societies are evidences of clearer views. But let us remember this was all

---

[49] Original: to beard the.

comparatively new in Whitefield's time, and let us give him the credit he deserves.

In short, I come to the conclusion that no man has ever done more good in his day and generation than the man who is the subject of this lecture. He was a true hero, and that in its highest and best sense. He did a work that will stand the fire, and glorify God, when many other works are forgotten. And for that work I believe that England owes a debt to his character which England has never yet paid.

And now, I hasten to a conclusion. I have set before you, to the best of my ability, Whitefield's time, and life, and religion, and preaching, and actual work. I have not extenuated his faults, to the best of my knowledge. I have not exaggerated his good qualities, so far as I am aware. It only remains for me to point out to you two great practical lessons which the subject appears to me to teach.

The amazing power that one single man possesses

Learn then, I beseech you, for one lesson, the amazing power that one single man possesses, when he is determined to work for God, and has got truth on his side.

Here is a man who starts in life with everything, to all appearance, against him. He has neither family, nor place, nor money, nor high connections on his side. His views are flatly opposed to the customs and prejudices of his time. He stands in direct opposition to the stream of public taste, and the religion of the vast bulk of ministers around him. He is as much isolated and alone, to all appearances, as Martin Luther opposing the Pope, as Athanasius resisting the Arians, as Paul on Mars' Hill. And yet this man stands his ground. He arrests public attention. He gathers crowds around him who receive his teaching. He is made a blessing to tens of thousands. He turns the world upside down. How striking these facts are!

Here is your encouragement, if you stand alone. You have no reason to be cast down and faint-hearted. You are not weak, though few, if God is with you. There is nothing too great to be done by a little company, if only they have Christ on their side. Away with the idea that numbers alone have power! Cast away the old vulgar error that majorities alone have strength. Get firm hold of the great truth that minorities always move the world. Think of the little flock that our Lord left behind him, and the one hundred and twenty names in that upper chamber in Jerusalem, who went forth to assault the heathen world! Think of George Whitefield assailing boldly the ungodliness which deluged all around him, and winning victory after victory! Think of all this. Cast fear away. Lay out your talents heartily and confidently for God.

Here, also, is your example, if you desire to do good to souls. Whether you become ministers, or missionaries, or teachers, never forget you must fight with Whitefield's weapons, if you wish to have any portion of

Whitefield's success. Never forget what John Wesley said was Whitefield's theology—"Give God all the glory of whatever is good in man: set Christ as high and man as low as possible, in the business of salvation. All merit is in the blood of Christ, and all power is from the Spirit of Christ."

Think not for a moment that earnestness alone will insure success. This is a huge delusion. It will do nothing of the kind. All the earnestness in the world will never enable a teacher of German theology to show you one Tinnevelly, or a teacher of semi-Popery one Sierra Leone. Oh, no! it must be the simple, pure, unadulterated Gospel that you must carry with you, if you are to do good. You must sow as Whitefield sowed, or you will never reap as he reaped.

Thankfulness for the present condition of the Church of England

Learn, in the last place, what abundant reasons we have for thankfulness in the present condition of the Church of England.

We are far too apt to look at the gloomy side of things around us, and at that only. We are all prone to dwell on the faults of our condition, and to forget to bless God for our mercies. There are many things we could wish otherwise in our beloved Church, beyond all question. There are defects we could wish to see remedied, and wounds we should gladly see healed. But still, let us look behind us, and compare the Church of our day with the Church of Whitefield's times. Look on this picture, and on that, and I am sure, if you do so honestly and fairly, you will agree with me that we have reason to be thankful.

We have bishops on the bench now, who love the simple truth as it is in Jesus, and are ready to help forward good works—bishops who are not ashamed to come forward in Exeter Hall, and lend their aid to the extension of Christ's Gospel—bishops who would have welcomed a man like Whitefield, and found full occupation for his marvelous gifts. Let us thank God for this. It was not so a hundred years ago.

We have hundreds of clergymen in our parishes now, who preach as full a Gospel as Whitefield did, though they may not do it with the same power—clergymen who are not ashamed of the doctrine of regeneration, and do not pronounce a minister a heretic, because he says to ungodly people, "You must be born again." Let us thank God for this. A man need not travel many miles now in order to find parishes where the Gospel is preached. When driven out of one parish church he can find truth in another. It was not so a hundred years ago.

We have thousands of laymen now, who are fully alive to the duties and responsibilities of members of a Protestant Church—laymen who rejoice in holding up the hands of evangelical ministers, and are righteously jealous for the maintenance and extension of evangelical truth. Let us thank God for this. It was not so a hundred years ago.

We have societies and agencies for evangelizing every dark corner of the earth in connection with our Church. We have wide and effectual doors of usefulness for all who are willing to labor in the Lord's vineyard. The difficulty now is, not so much to find openings for doing good, as to find men. Let us thank God for this. It was not so a hundred years ago.

Young men of the Church of England, I ask you to gather up these facts, and treasure them in your memories. They are facts. They cannot be gainsayed.[50] Treasure them up, I repeat. Look back a century, and then look around you, and then judge for yourselves whether you ought not to be thankful.

Beware, I beseech you, of that tribe of men who would fain[51] you to forsake the Church of England, and separate from her communion. There is a generation of murmurers and complainers in the present day, who seem to revel in picking holes—a generation that seems to forget that fault-finding is the easiest task in all the world—a generation that has no eyes to see the healthy parts in our body of priests,[52] but has a wonderfully quick and morbid scent for detecting its sores—a generation that is mighty to scatter, but impotent to build—a generation that would persuade churchmen to strain at gnats, but finds no difficulty itself in swallowing camels—a generation that would have you pull the old

---

[50] *Gainsayed* meaning to deny or contradict.
[51] *Fain* meaning to persuade.
[52] Original: our body ecclesiastic.

house down, but cannot offer you so much as a tent in its place: of all such men I say solemnly and affectionately—of all such men I warn you to beware. Listen not to them. Have no friendship with them. Avoid them. Turn from them. Pass away.

Let us not leave the good old ship, the Church of England, until we have some better reason than can at present be seen. What though she be old and weather-beaten! What though, in some respects, she may lack repair! What though some of the crew be not to be depended on! Still, with all her faults, the old ship is in far better trim than she was a century ago. Let us acknowledge her faults, and hope they may yet be amended. But still, with all her faults, let us stick by the ship!

When the Thirty-nine Articles of the Church of England are repealed, and the Prayer Book and Homilies so altered as to be unprotestantized—when regeneration and justification by faith are forbidden to be preached in her pulpits—when the Queen, Lords and Commons, and laity, have assented to these changes—in short, when the Gospel is driven out of the Establishment—then, and not till then, it will be time for you and me to go out; but, till then, I say, Let us stick by the Church!

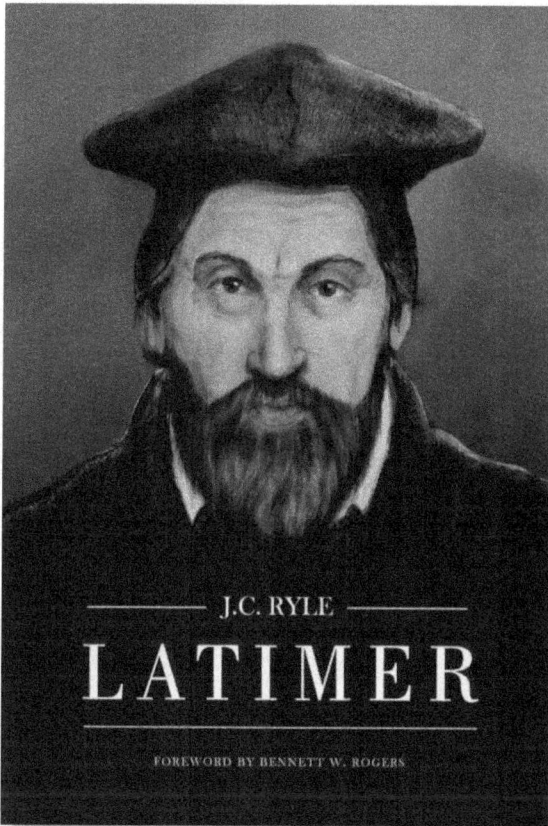

ISBN: 978-1-77526-338-8

Another of J. C. Ryle's short biographies on a man of God worthy of study. In this work he briefly examines the life and work of Bishop Hugh Latimer.

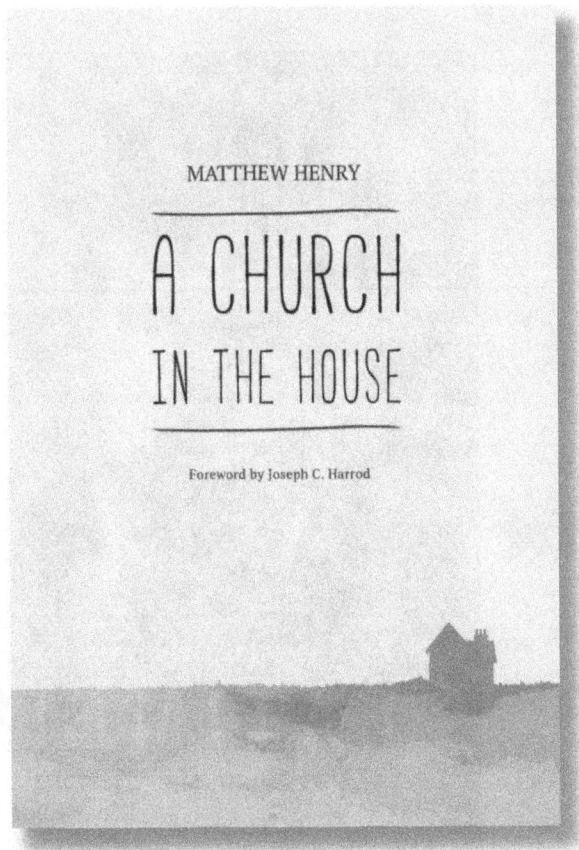

ISBN: 978-1-77526-333-3

Matthew Henry exhorts fathers to lead their homes well in family worship. This is an excellent resource for those who are aiming to be faithful in family discipleship.

ISBN: 978-1-77526-334-0

Fuller deals with the issue of backsliding: when genuine Christians lose their passion for Christ and his kingdom. This was not a theoretical issue for Fuller, therefore, and his words, weighty when he first wrote them, are still worthy of being pondered—and acted upon.

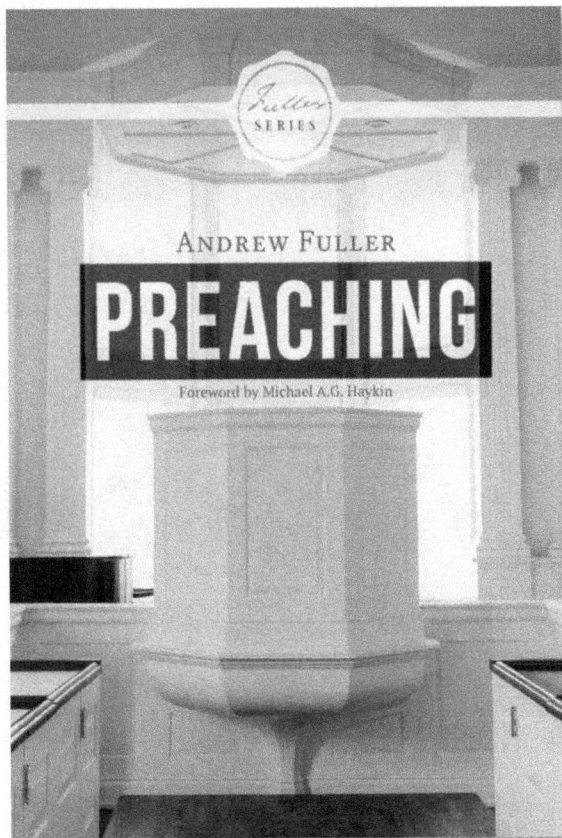

ISBN: 978-1-77526-336-4

Fuller wrote to encourage a young minister in sermon preparation and reading this work will be of great value to any preacher today.

ISBN: 978-1-77526-339-5

In the eyes of Fuller, Samuel Pearce (1766–1799) was the epitome of the spirituality of their community. In fact, in that far-off day of the late eighteenth century Pearce was indeed well known for the anointing that attended his preaching and for the depth of his spirituality. It was said of him that "his ardour ... gave him a kind of ubiquity; as a man and a preacher, he was known, he was felt everywhere."

Date Completed	Name

ABOUT
◨H&E Publishing

H&E Publishing is a Canadian evangelical publishing company located out of Peterborough, Ontario. We exist to provide Christ-exalting, Gospel-centred, and Bible-saturated content aimed to show God to be as glorious and worthy as He truly is.

We seek to provide rich resources that will equip, nourish, and refresh the Christian's soul. We desire to make available a variety of works that serve this purpose in the church. One key area of focus is to revive evangelicals of the past through updated reprints.

Notes:

Notes:

Notes:

Notes:

Notes:

Notes:

Notes:

Notes:

www.ingramcontent.com/pod-product-compliance
Lightning Source LLC
Chambersburg PA
CBHW031522040426
42445CB00009B/351

9 781989 174012